Makayla's Heart:
Moment by Moment

By

Dell R. Hyssong, Jr. and Holly Weiss

Makayla's Heart: Moment by Moment

ISBN: 978-1-935188-75-9

Edited by T.C. McMullen
Cover by Mark MacDonald
Interior design by T.C. McMullen

A Star Publish LLC Publication
www.starpublishllc.com
Published in 2015
Printed in the United States of America

Advance Praise

"...a strong message of healing with faith and belief as its foundation." — Diane Lunsford, *Feathered Quill Book Reviews*

"Joy at the birth of a first grandchild quickly turned into despair...overwhelmed under devastating possibilities, their faith shines forth in this touching story." — Barbara Anne Waite, author of *Elsie - Adventures of an Arizona Schoolteacher 1913-1916*

On behalf of our family, I would like to thank all those who prayed for my granddaughter, Makayla, and upheld all of us during some of the most difficult days we have ever faced. Your prayers, cards, gifts and expressions of love will always be remembered.

Dell R. Hyssong, Jr.

Makayla's Heart:
Moment by Moment

1

Everything's Fine

Makayla was three days old when the doctors told us, "She's not going to make it."

For months we had eagerly anticipated the birth of our first grandchild. No abnormalities showed up in pre-delivery ultrasounds. After Makayla was born, the doctors heard a swishing noise in her heart. She was sent to Maine Medical Center in Portland (two hours south of our home in Rockport) for an appointment with a pediatric cardiologist, Dr. Reyes. He immediately did an ultrasound.

Kelly, Makayla's mother and our daughter-in-law, didn't know a lot, but what she learned wasn't good.

"I'm sorry to tell you this. Makayla has over twenty tumors in and around her heart. One is blocking the blood flow to the aorta by 75%," said Dr. Reyes.

Kelly was so devastated when the doctor told her, she could barely speak. She called us, crying while she relayed the news. We stood stunned.

My wife, Susan, my son, Richard (Makayla's father) and I were not present when Kelly got that terrible news. We were scheduled to sing the entire week at a camp in northern Maine. Susan, Richard and I are a travelling singing trio booked to sing 250 concerts a year. Normally we consider this a blessing. That day we had to make tough decisions. We walked up to the conference director and cancelled the rest of our concerts for the week. He and his wife were kind enough to help us pack our equipment into our vans. Richard needed to be with his family and we couldn't bear to be away.

Frantically, we travelled the four hours home. I'll never forget the trip. I drove one car with Richard as my passenger. Susan followed in a second car. Richard desperately tried to reach Kelly on the phone to find out more information. He knew Makayla had been sent right from Dr. Reyes to a geneticist in the Portland hospital for more testing. We were six hours away from them at this point with absolutely no cell phone reception. Richard was silent with frustration and anxiety. You could cut the air with a knife. We drove. He dialed. We weren't sure if we would meet up with Kelly and the baby at the hospital or at home.

Finally, in the tiny town of Lincoln, Richard lurched forward in the passenger seat staring at his phone.

"Dad, I've got towers."

We immediately pulled over.

"What's happening?" Susan slammed her car door and ran to us.

Richard and I paced on the shoulder of the road. He had his left index finger stuck in his ear so he could hear Kelly. His cell phone was on speaker in his other hand clutched between his thumb and fourth finger. He pointed his finger in a "just-a moment" pose to silence our questions. Kelly was giving him results and statistics in between tears. Makayla would eventually be released to go home with her. All other details were hazy. We prayed as we drove the rest of the way to Rockport.

Three days before, we had experienced overwhelming joy and excitement at the birth of our granddaughter. Now, we all needed to prepare ourselves for the worst.

Because of our profession, our concerts and private lives are intricately interwoven. For weeks before Kelly was due, I worried we would be on the road instead of home when Makayla was born. Kelly's due date was July 29th. I wanted Richard to be with Kelly in Maine, but we were scheduled to sing in Delaware. Susan and I conferred frequently about cancelling some engagements. We had never cancelled before. Quite frankly, if we don't work we don't eat and we can't pay our bills. Our business supports Richard, his family, Susan and me. I thought about bringing in a substitute for Richard, but he is irreplaceable. In addition to providing harmony in the trio, he takes the solo on many songs, plays trombone and trumpet duets with me, and plays piano duets with Susan. I was stymied.

"You need more faith this will work out," I heard Susan say more than once.

On July 18, 2008 we sang in Port Clyde, Maine, just a few miles from our home. Kelly, uncomfortable in her ninth month of pregnancy, stayed home. After the service we dropped Richard off at their house.

Moments after we walked in our front door around ten PM, Richard called.

"Kelly's water broke. We're heading for the hospital."

He told us not to come right away. He would call us when she was closer to delivery. Dead tired, I slept. Susan stayed up and worried. (This occasionally got thrown in my face.) Another call and we hurried to the hospital where we waited with Kelly's parents in the room Kelly would occupy after delivery.

On Saturday, July 19, 2008 at 4:44 AM, Makayla Lynn Hyssong was born.

Shortly afterward, my cell phone rang. An array of emotions swept over me because the caller ID was Richard.

"Hey, Dad, Makayla's been born, but she doesn't look anything like you. She has hair!" Richard, my son, never misses an opportunity to crack a joke. Susan and I hurried to the nursery. Then things started to go south.

As we watched through the nursery window, the nurses' behavior got more and more peculiar.

"That's the fifth time," I told Susan when a second nurse pressed a stethoscope to Makayla's chest. She conferred with the first nurse and glanced over at us. Then they both gave our new granddaughter their full attention. They had Makayla under the light in an incubator against the back wall.

"What's going on?" Susan asked as we squinted through the nursery window. "Clearly something isn't right."

The nurses all stood huddled together with their faces turned away from us. Everything was very hush-hush. We wanted more information, but they were tied up checking Makayla and we couldn't catch their attention. Just then Richard joined us. He had left Kelly, who was in the delivery room getting stitched up. He said she was doing well.

"What's happening? You guys look scared to death."

Finally, the main nurse rushed past us."Your baby is fine. Trust us, we know what we're doing. The heartbeat is a little fast. Don't be alarmed."

"Hold it." I caught the nurse by the wrist. "We deserve to know what is going on. I haven't seen a doctor on the scene yet. You get a physician in here now or we will life-lift the baby to the Portland hospital."

"We see this all the time, sir. Don't worry." The expression on the nurse's face belied her attempt to calm us down.

"Well, I'm not convinced," Richard stated."It's obvious you are basically guessing. We want the on-call doctor. Now." His face was frozen and he couldn't take his eyes off his daughter.

"Certainly, Mr. Hyssong. We'll call the doctor immediately." The head nurse rushed off.

I felt helpless. Richard constantly ran back and forth between Kelly and the baby. "Hey, go see Kelly. Mom and I will stay here with Makayla." I held up my phone. "You'll know the minute we do when the on call doctor gets here." I put my arm around his shoulder, gave him a squeeze, and he took off to be with his wife.

Just as calm as could be a nurse came out and spoke to Susan. "Do you want to see the baby?"

I hadn't seen my wife move so fast in years. They didn't make Susan gown up or put gloves on. The nurses all disappeared. I watched through the glass as Susan talked to our granddaughter and touched her hand. I doubt Susan will ever forget their special time together.

Finally, the on call doctor arrived.

2

Day By Day

Several years prior, before we started performing full-time on the road, Susan had been called into our local school district to substitute for a special needs teacher. A boy with high-functioning autism needed individual attention. Richard and I greatly admired her dedication to this student. The child began to calm, to excel, and to learn quickly. Impressed with Susan's work, the family requested she stay on after the original teacher returned to school.

"So that's why I rushed over," the doctor told Richard outside the nursery door later that Saturday, when Makayla was less than a day old. "I recognized the name 'Hyssong' from when your mom cared for my son. What goes around comes around. Let me check out your daughter and I'll confer with you afterward. Why don't you join your wife and I'll come to her room when I'm done?"

Kelly at this point was completely oblivious to what was going on. I admired Richard for trying to shield her after the trauma of giving birth. He filled in a bit of the picture for his wife while we waited for the doctor.

The doctor pulled back the curtain in Kelly's room, rolled up her stethoscope, and put it in her pocket. "I detected an unusual sound in your daughter's heart. It's probably just a heart murmur. Many children have them, but to make sure, a second ultrasound might be in order. I've alerted your primary care physician. For now, just relax. She'll be fine."

"But we have concerts the next few days. Should we leave her?" I asked, completely at a loss for the right thing to do.

The doctor reassured us, told us to get some rest, and to keep our performance commitments. We had an engagement that very evening. Richard, who was stressed out, didn't want to go. Kelly convinced him that he should because her parents were staying with her.

"The concert's so close, you can be back to the hospital tonight. We'll be fine," Kelly said.

On Sunday, July 20, when Makayla was one day old, we sang another service in the morning. Richard returned to be with Kelly and the baby, while Susan and I started traveling to northern Maine for the week of engagements we wound up cancelling. The constant decisions about whether to perform or keep Richard home with Makayla and Kelly were emotionally wrenching. Richard and Kelly, afraid of what might happen, got no sleep that night. They held and watched their daughter because there was nothing else they could do for her. We had to wait for more tests.

On August 1, 2008, thirteen days after she was born, Makayla had the second heart ultrasound at Maine Medical Center. They also did a brain ultrasound through the soft spot in her skull. Richard, beside himself to get the results because we had to sing in Delaware the next day, jumped when the phone rang at 8:30 PM. Dr. Stephenson, their pediatrician, had Makayla's results.

"How serious is this?" Richard asked, nervously drumming his fingers on the end table.

Dr. Stephenson explained that in addition to the heart tumors there were clusters in the brain, but it was impossible to assess the extent until Makayla could have a brain MRI. This procedure could not be performed until September. She would have to be anesthetized for an extended period of time, which was dangerous for a child less than two months of age. We went to Delaware with a sick feeling in our stomachs, praying all the way. Kelly and her mother stayed home with Makayla. We all agreed if Makayla got worse we would immediately return home.

August 22. Makayla had an appointment with Dr. Reyes, pediatric cardiologist. He reported the blockage to her aorta was reduced from 75% to 55%. The tumors in her heart had not grown.

September 18. Appointment with Dr. Reyes. Makayla's heart was beating normally. Richard, Susan and I had been away from home for twenty-four days and were dying to get home to see her.

September 30. Makayla had the brain MRI. She was two months old.

Susan and I tried not to interfere. Richard and Kelly were spectacular parents and communicated with us about what was happening. But this day was big. We offered to drive them to the hospital for the test. They said no; then changed their minds. Our two-hour drive was the quietest I can remember.

Kelly started to cry when they put the mask over her

daughter's face to give her the anesthesia. An orderly ushered us into the waiting room. I walked the halls. I wanted to be a rock—to my son who had become a best friend, and to Kelly who I loved more like a daughter than a daughter-in-law. Outwardly, I wanted to appear strong. Inside, I was heartbroken.

They had a two o'clock appointment to see Dr. Rioux, a pediatric neurologist, who would explain the MRI results. His office was so busy they didn't get in until four PM. They filled us in shortly thereafter. He had ushered them into his office and asked them to sit down. Kelly cradled Makayla in her arms. He put the MRI pictures up for them to view, pointing to masses of white.

The results: Multiple tumors were in many areas of her brain, but they were benign, he explained.

His concern: The tumors were located in sections of Makayla's brain needed for speaking, balance, and learning. Surgery was not an option.

"Even if your daughter survives the heart blockage," he said grimly, "she will never be a normal child."

The days following were unbearable. We didn't know if Makayla was going to live or not. Would she be a healthy child or would she be severely disabled? Susan would cry herself to sleep, wake up the next morning and start crying again. Kelly held Makayla tight day and night, afraid of losing her. Richard paced the house, unable to sleep. He and Kelly kept putting their finger under the baby's nose trying to feel her breath to make sure she was still alive. I was frozen inside. I wanted to stay strong for them all, but I was hurting more than I could describe.

Finally, we got the diagnosis. Tuberous Sclerosis.

3

Don't Give Up

If you Google® Tuberous Sclerosis Complex you will find it is a genetically transmitted disorder causing non-cancerous tumors (technically called tubers) to form in various organs of the body. Many people live completely normal lives with the disorder, but they must be constantly monitored because of the tendency of the tubers to migrate to other organs and cause serious physiological malfunction. The disease primarily targets the kidneys, eyes, lungs, skin, heart and brain. Makayla's TSC affected the latter two. The major concern was the tuber (a tumor-like growth) lodged in her aorta, which cut off 75% of the blood flow to her heart.

The origin of the disorder's name comes from a tuber or a potato-like nodule in the brain pertinent to the condition. For the reader's clarity, we will refer to the growths as tumors.

Makayla's brain tumors were discovered ten days after she was born. The initial diagnosis concerning her heart burdened us beyond belief. The news about her brain felt like we were hit with an avalanche. We could barely face the possibility of the common effects of brain tumors:

seizures, intellectual disability, autism, or developmental delay.

Neither Kelly's initial ultrasound at eight weeks nor the subsequent one in March 2008 showed anything abnormal in the fetus. As far as we knew, Makayla in the womb was developing normally. What we did not know was the placenta, acting like a Petri dish, had been her enemy. In unborn babies with Tuberous Sclerosis Complex, the placenta spontaneously mutates the cells either from the moment of conception or as the embryo develops. The longer the baby stays in the womb, the more tumors can develop and grow. If Makayla had gone full term before her birth, the aortic tumor could have closed all blood flow to the heart. It is likely that Kelly's premature delivery saved Makayla's life.

Makayla's case was unique because Tuberous Sclerosis Complex is genetically transmitted. Dr. Stephenson referred Richard and Kelly to a geneticist. Both were tested for the gene in December, after Makayla's diagnosis. Neither parent had it. The doctors were stymied by this inconsistency. It wasn't that Makayla had TSC, but rather, how did she get it?

4

I Love You Son

In 2004 when Richard was still single, he purchased a home a short distance from ours. He wanted some security for the future and we all thought buying a house was a good investment. Frankly, a bit of space between us when we were home in Maine helped promote family sanity.

When he was twenty-one years old, Richard was invited to speak to a youth group of thirteen through eighteen-year-olds (or so he thought). Although Richard was comfortable singing in front of people, he had never given a talk to a group of young people in his life. He mulled over the problems of teenagers. Peer pressure, drinking, and bullying all worked their way into his prepared presentation.

To calm his jitters, he arrived several minutes early. His first surprise was when Kelly, a pretty brown-eyed girl he had met jogging, came into the room. His second was that the children trailing behind her were five to seven-year-olds. Other teachers ushered in their chattering charges. Seeing Kelly rattled him a bit. Realizing the content of his talk had to be changed, he quickly pointed it to a younger audience. Richard thinks well on his feet and it worked out fine.

He approached Kelly afterward. "Hey, Kelly, I really love Vanilla Bean Coolattas®. Care to join me for one?"

"Sure, I'll go," she replied.

He had to scramble then to make it happen. "Uh, my family's motor coach is the only transportation I've got. Would you mind driving?"

Kelly, who doesn't normally go anywhere on a whim, agreed. In Maine, everything closes down after seven PM so they had to drive a ways to find their Coolattas®. They rode around and, discovering Dunkin' Donuts® closed, kept going until they found a McDonalds®. No Coolattas® there, but they made do. They talked until the manager kicked them out at closing time.

When Richard talked about Kelly, he bubbled over. He had girlfriends over the years, but none of them were serious relationships. This time was different.

Their courtship did not wind up being an easy one. Kelly coached a junior varsity women's basketball team. Richard wanted to watch her team play one evening, but the game got snowed out. They planned a date after that, but Kelly got sick. In January, we had to leave for Florida. Emails sailed back and forth between them for several months. Even though we were only doing half of the concerts we do today, they were geographically separated. In March we returned to Maine.

We were a part of a large, sold out event at Messalonskee Performing Arts Center in Oakland. Richard invited Kelly to come. We were busy as usual selling CD's at our table. Kelly slipped in toward the back and stood there quietly.

Susan elbowed Richard, nodding in Kelly's direction. "I'm pretty sure that's Kelly."

Off he flew.

He called her the next day. They had dinner at Longhorn Steak House (still one of our favorites for sentimental reasons). They kept dating. Susan and I were pretty sure he had met his future wife.

In July, I was certain of it. Richard does most of our bookings. When he insisted we hold open October 1, 2005, a Saturday, I suspected that was the day he wanted to marry Kelly. I was right.

We wanted to make sure she knew what she was getting into. A performer's life isn't easy. She and Richard would be travelling quite a bit in our motor home with Susan and me. To give Kelly a taste of her new life, we invited her to come along for a couple of weekends. In the motor home, the ladies slept in the bedroom. Richard and I took the couches in the living area. Kelly and Susan prepared meals together. She fit right in, helping us carry our equipment and setting it up. I think that was the first time she heard us sing. She was very supportive afterwards. We had some big events in the south and she flew down to see us. Kelly was practically already part of the family. We gently told her we had a venue the day after their wedding. She graciously understood. We'd passed the first part of the "in-laws" test.

I was honored when Kelly and Richard asked me to perform the ceremony. The rehearsal went off without a hitch. Blue sky and sunshine greeted us on their wedding day. Dressed in our best, Richard, his best man and I sat downstairs in the fellowship hall, listening to the music playing upstairs. I had pastored this church for nine years before we decided to go singing on the road full-time. I must have performed a hundred weddings but this one felt different. I was incredibly nervous, but tried to act calm for my son.

Memories of Richard's childhood flooded back to me. I used to pass a football back and forth down the street with him in the mornings on his way to the school bus. He played varsity baseball in high school and was a great left-handed hitter. Susan and I went to as many of his games as possible. At home, he practiced constantly with a whiffle ball and bat.

One day I noticed him, bat in hand, in the front yard. "Richard, do your practicing in the back yard, not out here," I called to him from the front door.

Just as I got back in the house I heard a crack. His ball went right through the picture window of the living room. He mysteriously disappeared somewhere safe in the neighborhood. I'm sure all of our neighbors heard me calling for him loud and clear.

"Dad, I hit that ball so hard, I can't believe you aren't proud of me," he justified later when he finally came home and cleaned the glass off the carpet.

Our family's favorite game is still baseball.

Richard was in all the musicals in high school, mostly playing lead roles. I recalled his performance in "The Sound of Music," while the clock ticked down the moments until the wedding ceremony. Richard's best man broke my reverie.

"It's time."

We mounted the stairs to the sanctuary. I took my place as the officiate. The maid-of-honor processed down the center aisle to Pachelbel's "Canon in D." Then the organist, signaling the appearance of the bride, pulled out the brass stops and played the majestic Trumpet Voluntary. Kelly was breathtakingly beautiful that day. The ceremony went off without a hitch.

In my nervousness, however, I neglected to have the marriage license signed. The maid of honor was still there so she signed for Kelly, but Richard's best man had already left. One of my friends had come all the way to Maine from Rhode Island for the wedding. He consented to be Richard's witness. We've laughed about it many times since. When we see my friend, he always reminds Richard that if it weren't for him Richard wouldn't legally be married.

Married. Letting your kids go is perhaps the hardest thing for a parent. If we really love them, we raise them to be prepared for life and love. As Richard and Kelly kissed and turned to go down the aisle to their new lives, I knew ours would never be the same.

But I'll tell you one thing. Richard and I have always shared a strong love. I can honestly say, "I love you son, I love you."

5

This Is the Day

We were at a juncture where we had to choose to go on or to dissolve into despair. Susan, the member of our family least known to our followers, demonstrated how we would get through.

Our next concert was in a white clapboard church in Maine. Church folk were busy readying the food table for the social hour planned in the fellowship hall afterward. Coffee perked in the kitchen. People milled around as we set up our equipment. Susan put the finishing touches on the table where we would sell CD's during a break in the concert. We loved this portion of our engagements. We got to catch up with followers, old friends, and new acquaintances as we shared refreshments and conversation. This one-on-one connection always bolstered us. We tried to listen and comfort those who shared their stories with us.

Her setup done, I watched Susan pick Makayla up from her pink Minnie Mouse car carrier and head back to the coach to change into performance clothes.

A woman with black hair pulled into a ponytail

materialized on Susan's heels. "Babies die, you know," she blurted. Susan headed for the door. "You'd better prepare yourselves." The encroachment made my skin crawl. My instincts told me to jump in to save Susan, but something in her determination held me back. I knew my wife was a rock.

Susan strode doggedly forward, trying to ignore the intrusion. She held our granddaughter tight and kept walking out to the parking lot. I'm sure she could hear the woman's pounding footsteps as she followed Susan right to our motor home and never let up.

At a higher volume and with a more abrasive tone, she said, "That baby is not going to make it!"

Susan, who never lashed out at people, pulled Makayla protectively back in one arm. My wife's face was red and her neck blotched with shades of purple. She turned to the pursuer, and shook her finger vigorously in ponytail-lady's face.

"I don't know how you feel, but I know my God is more powerful than that!"

Later when we went to bed, her temper gone, questions tumbled out.

"Why would God allow this to happen to Makayla?"

I turned to her. "Why not? Everyone goes through tough times. God's in control and He's always been so good to us."

I said it, but deep down inside I guess I had the same question. Why would God bring this into our lives? Embarking on this exciting music ministry was why I left the pastorate. Our concerts were going well. Invitations for more poured in. People were turning their hearts and lives to God. Would this be the end of it?

"Susan, if Makayla turns out to be a special needs

child, Richard and Kelly will need our help. That means you and I can't be on the road anymore than Richard can. Maybe we've done all we can in this endeavor and we need to turn our attention to them," I said, knowing how foreign it seemed to how we dreamed our lives would proceed.

"Yes, Dell, but from what the doctors tell us, we won't know about Makayla for awhile. In the meantime, we will keep praying. If God wants us to stop our ministry, He'll show us. Until He does, I'm not going to let one woman's doubts stop me. How about you?" That night we decided God wanted us to continue.

6

The Bond of Love

Christmas in the Smokies." We love this annual event in Pigeon Forge, Tennessee, gateway to the Great Smoky Mountains. Many artists and groups share in the entertainment portion and we enjoy renewing old acquaintances. Christmas lights and decorations adorn the area. People pour in for a holiday vacation filled with Christian music, good food, and onstage hilarity. Staying put for a few days is an extra perk for our family. At its inception, "Christmas in the Smokies" was a three-day event, however each year days are added because it is always sold out.

Playing with the audience has become one of our trademarks. They love to hear Richard and I pick on each other. We often wonder if they enjoy that part more than our music.

In December 2008 despite our personal difficulties, we whipped out our onstage persona. Susan, the creative coordinator of our performance wardrobe, chose the red, white and black ensembles. To be festive for the final night, I went with my black suit and red pocket-handkerchief. Richard wore black dress pants and a black and grey pinstriped vest. Both of us sported red ties. Susan pulled it all together with a black skirt, white blouse, and a red jacket with black velvet buttons.

We stood backstage until we heard, "Put your hands together to welcome the Hyssongs!"

After two opening songs I introduced the trio members and explained that because of the number of concerts we do a year, we travel as a family in a motor coach.

"Our son, Richard, has been singing with us since he was thirteen years old and I couldn't be more pleased to have him by my side," I announced that night as I do at every concert. When I emcee at concerts, Richard tends to back up on the stage. I can't see him and I'm never sure what he's going to do or say.

Richard, adept at putting on the I'm-not-too-smart-comedian mask, fueled the banter. "Oh yeah," he stepped forward and took my microphone right out of my hand. "I mean travelling with your parents day after day... after day...after day...I mean it's just wonderful."

Jumping in after his zinger, I added, "This is a good time for you to play 'When the Saints Go Marching In', don't you think?" Audiences go wild when Richard plays this on his trombone. He gives it a little fancy footwork and lots of panache.

"Whatever you say, Dad."

Moving closer downstage while he got his trombone, I confided in the audience. "You know, when a family travels together like we do, I think it's important that we act as a democracy and make decisions together." Chuckles of enjoyment came back from the people listening. Humorous adlibbing always went over big.

He cut me off. "A democracy? This is a dictatorship!"

I turned on my innocent hurt face. "How could you

say such a thing and embarrass me in front of all these people?" To the audience I said, "We all have families and family disagreements, right? Would you mind just not listening for a minute while I take care of this one?"

Richard rushed up, pumping his thumb at me. "See? He's even telling *you* what to do!"

I made a space of two inches between my thumb and index finger and shook my hand at him. "Sometimes, Richard, you are that close to an idiot."

With his famous sheepish grin, he backed far away from me. His timing was perfect. "No way do I want to be that close."

Pause.

"Think I should play now, Dad?"

The audience roared. They eat it up when we pick on each other. We use this trademark in every concert. People not only expect it. It is anticipated.

We programmed our popular new release as the next to last song that night. Richard had the verse as a solo. While he sang a young girl stopped tickling her brother's ear. A coughing woman became silent and leaned forward in her chair. A dozing grandfather suddenly woke up and cocked his head. I realized my son had something voice teachers can't teach and performers can't learn no matter how much they practice. Richard has an innate quality when he sings. Magnetism.

Richard and I went out exercising at 7:30 the next morning.

"They really liked the 'close to an idiot bit' last night. Good thinking, Dad. We should use it again."

Richard playfully kicked a stone off the path. We try

to walk three miles every day, using the time to plan and commiserate on our trio's ministry. We stopped at a diner for breakfast.

The breakfast thing is a ticklish subject. As brilliant as Richard is onstage, he tends to be forgetful about those little everyday things. He says, "Dad, I forgot my wallet," nine times out of ten on our mornings together, but that time he offered to take care of the bill. Over our meal, we discussed the day's plans, projects we were implementing over the next six months, and what to record for our next CD.

Richard and I are much more than father and son or two-thirds of The Hyssongs trio. We are business partners. People see us together on stage, but they may not realize how much work goes into what we do. We respect each other. We love each other. We have each other's back. We feel blessed to have our ministry. Prayer surrounds all of our decision-making.

The division of labor works well. Richard books most of our concerts and takes care of social media. He calls promoters, pastors and radio DJs to bolster the popularity of our songs. Choosing what songs suit our trio best is his forte. He strongly feels that if the lyrics speak to our lives they will touch others. He and our producer schedule dates for the trio to record vocals and for the band and strings to lay down their tracks. He is a genius at coming up with innovative ideas to keep our ministry fresh. He is our people person.

I am the manager of The Hyssongs. Decision-making falls to me, frequently, after consultation with Susan and Richard. I order the line-up of songs, banter, and narration of our concerts. We have to tailor our program for the specific audience we sing to and that can be tricky. I pay bills, keep track of finances, and do all of our banking. Since we are only home a few weeks out of the year, this is sometimes a juggling act. Keeping the motor home and generator running and deciding how we will get from one venue to another is a challenging task.

What to those reading our itinerary may appear to be a Hyssongs day off is really a concentrated time of planning and negotiating the future of our ministry. We are associated with a demanding industry. We often start at 7 AM and don't wrap up until ten at night. All day both of our cell phones ring incessantly. Staying in contact with each other is essential to keep us both informed. Questions bounce around our office all day.

"What are you hearing? What's going on? What's new?"

Susan and Kelly have important roles as well. You'll find out more about them when I tell you about our life in our road coach.

7
Stay Close to Me

After "Christmas in the Smokies," we travelled back to Maine. Makayla had two doctor appointments. Dr. Rioux wanted to see how the brain tumors were affecting her neurological progress. Dr. Reyes would check for blood flow and heartbeat.

"Our family does our fair share of waiting for medical news," I said to Susan who was checking her grocery list from the passenger seat of our van.

"Normally I find our busyness a challenge, but today I'm grateful for it," she replied. "My mind is always on Makayla, but a bit of respite is good. No sense worrying until we hear the results. Today I have a feeling we will get good news."

I squeezed her hand and she headed into the store. If it weren't for Susan's organizational skills about everyday details, my family would be lost. I relaxed, my head back against the headrest. My mind wandered back to right after Makayla was born.

Our family bonded together, but felt isolated from other people after we cancelled all of those concerts at Living

Waters Bible Conference. People had always bolstered us with financial, prayer, and emotional support. We knew they would embrace us when we reached Rockport and got the word out.

Without our knowledge, the minute we left the conference grounds to return home, the director's daughter, good friends with Richard and Kelly, had sent out a mass email to congregations all over the country.

"Baby Makayla Hyssong has a problem with her heart. Please pray." The email was succinct, but powerful. While we drove, people all over the country were praying for Makayla.

Just before we reached home that Tuesday, we refueled outside of Rockport.

"We heard you guys were headed home. A man stopped for gas an hour ago and told me your little granddaughter was very sick. He knows you from attending your concerts. He said when he heard it on the radio, he pulled right over and prayed."

Sam, the owner, wouldn't let me pay for my gas that day. He pressed the bills back into my hand. "I'm sure you have a better place to use this."

People heard it on the radio? We hadn't told anyone outside our family! We were astounded to hear that news of Makayla's heart issues had gone viral before we even got home.

Sunday, July 27, 2008. Our concert in Eastport, Maine, a little over a week after Makayla was born, came flooding back to me. Eastport is a beautiful coastal town. People swarmed into the church after hearing our news. The church had to scramble to find enough lobsters to serve at the pre-concert dinner. People came, enfolding us with compassion and prayer support.

We put our despair about Makayla's precarious future on the shelf, substituting a good face for the concert. After a big opener and a trumpet-trombone duet, "Stay Close to Me" was next on the program. Reserved and intense, Richard started his solo. His expression had a guarded intensity I'd not seen before. My nerves were on alert. Something about music expresses a singer's soul more than the words alone. We knew these words were coming from his heartbreak:

Lord, I knew a time like this would someday come my way,
When in disbelief I'd watch my whole life change.

When Susan and I joined in on the chorus, he turned away from the audience and dabbed his eyes. He blinked back tears on verse two. Suddenly he slumped over his microphone. I was afraid he would pass out. Susan stopped the music.

Even though most people in the audience knew what was happening with us, I explained Makayla's health issues to the crowd. I've done that every concert since. We took a short break, regrouped, and finished the program.

"Why?" Richard flopped onto our sofa after the concert. Kelly, next to him, held Makayla. He stood up and paced. "Why Makayla? Here I am singing on the road for Christ and my baby girl fights for her life every minute of every day!" Susan rushed to put her arms around him.

"You ask 'why?'" I said. "I ask, 'why not Makayla?' God doesn't pick and choose the shoulders on which hardship will fall. He promises to be with us, no matter what our lot. I have my own questions, Richard. But this I firmly believe. If it hadn't been Makayla it could just as well have been another child. We have to pray for faith and healing. We soldier on and do the ministry He gave us. If Makayla reaches a point where we can no longer continue, then we stop. For now, we have to treat her as if she will live."

"Treat her as if she will live. Mom keeps saying the same thing."

Day after day I watched Richard and Kelly hold back the tears. When our kids are little and they fall off a bike we can pick them up, kiss it, and make it better. At this point, I felt helpless because I could do nothing to help except listen and pray. My sense of inadequacy frustrated me beyond belief.

In time, we all came to realize that God allowed this in our lives. We struggled with the uncertainty and the hurt, but we knew that God would bring us through in the end.

Richard called, waking me from my memories. "We got great news from the doctors, Dad! Tell Mom. Kelly and I are on our way over to fill you in. Get a bottle warm for Makayla, will you? She's hungry!"

Joyfully, we posted the doctor appointments results on our website. The neurologist said she continued to develop normally. The cardiologist reported that the amount of blockage from the tumor in her aorta was reduced from 55% to 20%. As they had done since her birth, they warned us to get her to a hospital immediately if her lips turned blue or if she had random bleeding. So far, she had none of these symptoms. Things were looking up.

Because Makayla's heart had improved so much, Dr. Reyes cleared her to travel with us to Florida where we would continue to minister over the winter. We received referrals for pediatric cardiologists in the Orlando area.

We were overjoyed, but realized we had to ride over another bump in the road. Kidney tumors are common with Tuberous Sclerosis children. Makayla's first kidney ultrasound was scheduled for Christmas Eve day.

Now that people knew about Makayla's health, they wanted to see her on stage. The reassurance that she was still alive gave people hope. We knew people all over were praying for her. The reports of her consistent improvement elated us, but we were still cautious.

Much to Richard's dismay because he always seemed allergic to housework, Susan had him washing dishes after a family dinner. While she wiped them dry, she asked, "What if you sang to Makayla during a concert?"

He jerked his head in her direction, as if lightening struck him. "Mom, what a terrific idea! Kelly, what do you think? It wouldn't hurt her. I'd be holding her the entire time."

Kelly wrapped her arms around him from behind. "I've always known my mother-in-law is smart. We've been trying to encourage Makayla's development and to give her different kinds of stimulation. I'm sure she'd love it. Will you be able to get through it, hon?"

"Absolutely. My hope meter is higher than it's been for four months."

At our next concert, Kelly held Makayla as usual for family introductions. When I asked the audience if they would like Richard to sing to his daughter, they applauded and cheered. He took the baby carefully from Kelly, sat on a stool, and held her on his knee. His song was a beautiful petition for God to make him a good father.

Makayla glanced at her dad when he started to sing. After five seconds, she completely ignored him! She twisted her body to and fro listening to our monitors, squinting into the spotlights, and watching her grandma adjusting the soundboard controls. Richard beamed at Kelly, who waited offstage in the wings. My granddaughter was alert and inquisitive. She came to life, acting like a normal four-month-old baby. Far outweighing the doctor reports, her behavior gave us a harbinger of hope.

8

Every Step I Take

More hope came with the news that Makayla's kidney ultrasound was normal. Unfortunately, optimism doesn't pay medical bills. We grappled with the cost of Makayla's tests. We still worried if she would live and what her life would be like. How could we pay for her care? The financial demands would be staggering, especially if she turned out to be a special needs child.

People rallied around us now that they knew our circumstances. God provided for us in miraculous, wonderful ways. We felt we were dipping into a trove of love.

Our followers creatively sent help, each in their own manner. The pastor of our church gave Richard and Kelly a gas card. Another couple sent an ice cream gift certificate so they could treat themselves after doctor visits. One day, a gift card to Wal-Mart® showed up anonymously. We received cards, letters, and pink prayer shawls in the mail, many from people we didn't even know. Those kindnesses can never be forgotten.

When we told Makayla's story at concerts, people offered to pray for her and shared stories of their own.

Children with all kinds of disabilities summoned our attention. We weren't sure if we had never noticed them before, or perhaps we were more sensitized to them and their families now that we were in the middle of it.

With compassion written all over his face, the pastor from a church in Tennessee approached Richard after a concert. "Does your daughter have Tuberous Sclerosis?"

"Yes, how did you know?"

"That's exactly what my nine-year-old son had. He always had a rapid heartbeat."

"How's your son doing?"

"He died a few months ago while he was playing outside."

To hear that someone else had lost a child to the same condition as Makayla really shook us. Worse than that, we felt so bad for even asking. We couldn't imagine the grief we stirred up in him.

You might assume when people hear a performing group; the more lasting impression is the music. In our case, Makayla's story was the most compelling message and was sending out beams of hope. We were amazed at how many people in this world had sick loved ones and needed the balm of meeting a child whose health was improving.

Food aromas had a funny way of getting to me. I'd read that smell more than any of our other senses help people associate things that happen in their lives. One Tuesday night Susan and I were home in Rockport. The aroma of meatloaf and baked potatoes came from the oven. She was working her usual cooking magic. The smells took me back to the last evening Susan cooked the same meal way back in September, after Dr. Rioux told Richard and Kelly about all of Makayla's brain tumors.

Richard had bought Makayla a bouncy seat in Delaware before we got home for that MRI. He had tears in his eyes when he paid for it. He excitedly took it out of the box to show us. The plush fabric was a neutral tan color with contrasting off white where the baby would lie. An oval pillow cradled the head and the baby could play with toys hanging from a mobile overhead. The seat gently rocked, vibrated, and played music. None of us knew if we would see Makayla again, but that gift seemed to calm and comfort Richard. The poor guy had to wait two weeks for us to finish traveling so he could see how his daughter enjoyed it.

Susan and I were three bites into our meatloaf when the phone rang.

"Dad, she moved her leg!"

"What? Makayla?"

"I was sitting on the stool in the kitchen." Words tumbled out of Richard so fast I could barely keep up with him. "Makayla was in her bouncy seat right next to me. I told her I loved her. Then I got an idea. I picked up my left foot and tapped her right foot. Then I don't know why, I touched my right toe to her left. Guess what? She smiled!"

As the words spilled out of him, he told me how he kept doing this alternate foot thing faster and faster.

Susan was dying to hear what our son was saying. After he hung up, I told her the whole thing. "He played with her for a minute, then she started actually copying him. He'd pick up his right foot and she'd pick up her left. She was smirking the whole time. They kept going faster and faster like it was a game."

"So three hours after we heard she might never

function, Makayla moved her legs?" Susan asked, wide-eyed. "She was mirroring him and having fun!"

"Here's the best part," I said. "He stopped the tapping. A moment later she raised a leg as if to say 'Daddy, I'm not done with this game yet.' He and Kelly must be elated."

I put my arms around my wife, realizing Richard and Kelly were probably doing the same thing. Dumfounded, we felt joy surging through us. God had given us many gifts through this experience but this was the best of all.

My shirt was wet with Susan's tears. When she finally raised her head she said, "So she danced with her daddy!"

After I heard about Makayla and Richard dancing, my fears about Richard's emotional and spiritual condition lessened considerably. The next day we were all together preparing for a concert. Richard explained to Susan and me how calm Kelly and he both felt that morning because of Makayla's new reaction to stimulation. For the first time, he had not reached his finger under Makayla's nose to check her breathing. We had gone from despair to elation within that one MRI-day. The four longest hours of our lives brimmed over with a roller coaster of emotions. Kelly, Susan, Richard and I wrapped our arms around each other. Our family hug was like harmony consecrated with tears.

"I think the 'can't keep your feet still' bit is appropriate tonight, Richard, how about you?"

He gave me a high-five and flashed a smile. "You got it. I am bursting with enthusiasm. I feel so much joy inside!"

Our third song was really peppy. Frolicking around the stage, Richard gushed with emotional energy as he sang.

"Have you ever noticed that Richard can't keep his feet still when he sings?"

This elicited laughter and shout outs of "Go, Richard," from the audience. People were on his side this time. (We never knew on any occasion which one of us would win sympathy.)

"When he was a kid, I used to threaten to nail his feet to the floor." Boos for me from the crowd.

"Yes, Dad, you sure did."

"He's never been diagnosed before..."

"Oh, come on."

"...Or anything like that, but I've always kind of wondered if he had that ADD stuff."

The audience roared when he quipped, "That's nothing, folks. My dad has AARP."

9

A Great Calm

"Dad, Kelly wrecked the van!" Richard's strident voice was on the other end of the distress call.

"Oh, great," Susan moaned.

"Is everyone all right?" I asked.

"Yes, Makayla is strapped into her car seat and we're just a bit shook."

We had just packed up after an outdoor event in a large tent. At the end of the long driveway, Susan and I waited for the kids, with our RV in park.

Without a clue of what "wrecking the car" meant, I jumped out and ran back to help them. I was more worried about my family than the minivan.

I put my hand on Kelly's arm. "Are you sure you are okay?"

"Yes, I'm fine. I'm sorry, Dell. I think I ran over a spike or something." Kelly sounded horrified. "I didn't want Richard to drive because he was dead on his feet."

I surveyed the damage. Somehow Kelly had backed over a big iron tent pole. It pulled the front fender and bumper almost completely off. We didn't need this. In four hours we were expected at our next engagement. I bit my tongue so I wouldn't say something I'd regret later. Kelly and I have never had harsh words since the day she married Richard and I wasn't about to give her a hard time then. Anyone can have an accident.

"Hey, can I help? I can give you a tow." A sandy-haired man in his forties called to us as he strode up the gravel driveway.

"Thanks, but we'll need more than a tow. We need to get it fixed soon and the damage looks pretty bad." I banged my fist against the bent fender.

"Don't worry. I own a body shop." He pointed to a large green garage on the same property. "If you let me rip off the rest of the fender, then I can move your vehicle."

Two hours later, the van fixed and painted, we caravanned to our next singing destination.

"Richard is a trip. You have to work overtime to keep my son calm, don't you?" Susan teased Kelly while they sorted lights, darks, and bleach loads at a Laundromat in Kentucky. "You're always at peace, never complaining, despite this crazy life we lead."

"I love our life. We're reaching people for Christ."

"That's what keeps us going. I'm not sure I could handle all of this otherwise."

"Makayla's first birthday is coming up and I praise God she's doing well. After her party, I really have to buckle down and work on my teaching recertification." Kelly had taught junior high school math prior to travelling with us and her current goal was to homeschool Makayla.

"Math and science, right?" Susan said.

"Teaching math and science. Once I pass the tests, I'm recertified for another five years."

"You carry a lot on your shoulders. I'm not sure I could concentrate to study after the year you've had."

"I'm not sure I could do everything you do after the year we've been through."

With mutual respect, they silently folded the first load to come out of the dryer.

We always happily returned to our home in Rockport, Maine. The Penobscot coastal area is known for its lobster industry, tourist attractions, and art galleries. We were only able to enjoy it for few days at a time sprinkled in between our travels each year. Richard and family lived a few miles south of us. The five of us enjoyed a convivial family life while we travelled in our forty-foot coach, but we all looked forward to the privacy we had at home in Maine.

One month before Makayla turned two, Richard took Kelly out for dinner to celebrate Kelly's birthday. Susan and I babysat Makayla. We took her to a park where she promptly wore us out, dashing from the slides to the swings and back again. With zeal she explored every opportunity for fun. We managed to pry her from the playground with promises of ice cream. Licking her vanilla ice cream cone with rainbow sprinkles was the only time she stopped running or talking.

"And the doctors doubted she would ever walk or talk..." Susan broke off. She reached back to squeeze Makayla's leg and was greeted with an ice-cream-face-grin.

Kelly and I had a meeting the next day to sift through some layout designs for our new CD.

"Before we get going, I have to show you some pictures." She swiped through a few on her cell phone and told me about their date the night before. After dinner they had driven to the Rockland Harbor and walked along the path by the waterfront that leads to the breakwater.

"Thanks for babysitting. We needed the time alone. We walked on the rocks the whole mile out to the breakwater lighthouse. We smelled salt water, heard the sea gulls, and listened to the water lapping."

Kelly always had a serenity about her. Her calm was a good balance for Richard, but that morning she was especially tranquil.

"Remember our visit to Dr. Reyes in December?"

"How could I forget," I said. "He tested Makayla and all of her heart tumors had shrunk by seventy-five percent!"

"I think Richard and I never really absorbed it until last night. We'll probably always worry when she runs, but she is completely able to. The doctor encourages her to be active. She's playful and communicative—and joyous! The closer we got to that lighthouse, the more we thanked God. Then we sat down on the rocks, held hands, and watched the colors in the sky. We felt so much peace."

"God has done wonders for our little girl."

"And for you, Dell, and the trio. You are able to keep ministering."

"Richard, please slow down. You don't need to rush."

"Dr. Rioux said he is going to test her on colors," he said as he put the pedal to the metal. "I'm rushing."

"But we allowed an extra half hour," Kelly said, checking her watch. "We have plenty of time."

"Are you going to bring that up again about how when I drove you to the hospital you said I was going too fast? And then when I ran into the ER for a wheelchair, you told me to calm down, that you were fine?" They played this game frequently with mutual enjoyment.

"As I recall, you phoned ahead for the wheelchair. And I was perfectly fine. I loved you for it, but you were completely frantic that night."

"You were eight centimeters dilated! I remembered from the birthing class that the birth process starts when the mother is at ten centimeters." He pulled into a parking space at the medical center. Kelly chuckled when she showed him her watch. They were a half hour early. As it turned out, December 15, 2010 was a mighty big day.

"Okay, little lady, let's see how you are today." Dr. Rioux, the pediatric neurologist, gave Makayla a little yellow duck to play with while he gently talked to her.

After she warmed up to him, he showed her a piece of cloth with three colored circles on it.

"Makayla, can you point to the green color for me?" She did without hesitating.

"And the blue?" Nailed that one too.

After further tests and a good bit of conversation with Makayla, he kept nodding his head, writing on her chart, but not saying a word.

Unable to keep his cool for another minute, Richard asked, "How did she do?"

We posted what the doctor told them on our website. Makayla at age two-and-a-half years was ahead of children her age in communication and skills. Colors were not normally mastered until a child reached the age of three.

"I kept asking her to stack up the blue blocks and then the green blocks and she wouldn't do it," Richard said, mystified.

"She was playing you, Richard." Kelly laughed with relief. "All this time, she's been playing us both. She could be, perhaps, as stubborn as her father."

10

While This Blessing's Being Made

Remarkable. We kept repeating the word to each other after the news moved through the family that Makayla knew her colors and was accelerated for her age. Later in the afternoon, she went to her pediatric cardiologist for her yearly checkup. The tumors in her heart as shown on the MRI results had been reduced to the size of tiny dots. We posted all of this on our website and thanked our followers for their prayers.

Here are a few more website posts for 2011:

Feb 28, 2011.
Our long awaited hymns project is released.

March 29, 2011.
Our new trio CD, "God Still Can" is now available.

July 19, 2011.
Happy Third Birthday, Makayla!

October 8, 2011.
Kelly and Richard are expecting their second child, a boy.

Kelly went to the pediatric cardiologist and everything looks fine with the baby's heart.

Our new grandson was due to arrive January 27, 2012. Kelly's father, Dennis, stayed with her for weeks, while our trio ministered in Florida. Every time the phone rang, we wondered if it was Kelly going into labor. Richard had scheduled two different times to fly home, trying to nail down the actual birth, but never hit the timing right. Makayla, in Maine with Momma, was getting antsy as well.

"I want us to go down to Florida to be with Daddy," she said on numerous occasions.

Kelly went into labor January 23 at 4:30 AM. She promptly put the plan she and Richard had worked out into place. She woke her father to take her to the hospital and called Richard's cousins, Bob and Stephanie, to babysit Makayla. Carolee, Kelly's mother, was on her way to be with her daughter in the hospital. Kelly's family kept us in the loop about what was happening and when. Richard was quite bummed out that he couldn't be there for the birth, but the second of his scheduled flights meant that he could see his family a few days after his son was born.

Kelly and Richard did their utmost to prepare Makayla for when Momma would deliver the baby. They explained that Stephanie and Bob (Richard's third cousins) would care for her while her mother went to the hospital. After Momma came home, her parents would stay with Kelly, Makayla, and the baby.

When Makayla peeked out of her bedroom, she saw Bob and Stephanie walking through the front door. She knew exactly what was happening. Dennis whisked Kelly off to the hospital.

"Momma said she wants you and Bob to clean my room," Makayla informed Stephanie. So they cleaned her room. Kelly had never given this directive, but when our three-year-old granddaughter saw the opportunity, she took it. Bob, Stephanie and Makayla watched Veggie Tales movies to pass the rest of the time.

At 9:32 AM on January 23, 2012, Dell Richard Hyssong IV, a perfectly healthy baby, was born. Kelly's parents took lots of pictures so that we wouldn't miss out on anything. They ushered Makayla in to meet her new brother.

"He's so tiny," she whispered. Richard was wrapped in a blue flannel blanket. She gingerly fingered it, never taking her eyes off his face.

Traditionally, the baby's mother and father have a celebratory lunch on the day the baby and mother leave the hospital. Since Richard couldn't be there, Kelly decided to have her lunch with Makayla. They ordered food from the cafeteria and ate in Momma's room. After their meal, Kelly and baby were released. Makayla was so excited about her new baby brother, she could barely keep still in her car seat.

A flooded basement greeted them when they reached home, but my cousin, who we all call Uncle Skip, came right over and fixed it. Water in the basement had no chance of dampening the rejoicing we felt. We were blessed to have a new baby in the family with no trace of Tuberous Sclerosis.

Throughout 2012, Richard and I were plagued with colds and asthma—not a great thing for singers. On this particular occasion, my physician prescribed an inhaler that gave me great relief. We were fortunate that we could call our family doctor no matter where we were in the country and he'd work out something with the local pharmacy.

"Call the doctor, Richard." I couldn't count the number of times I'd suggested this to my son. Ignoring me, he dug in his heels and checked the texts on his cell phone. I was driving, trying to concentrate on the road. I'd hear him grunt or laugh, see him nod his head, and make comments back to the text.

"What's going on? Is it a church confirming? Is the mixing coming along okay on the new CD?" Every prompt I offered was met with silence.

"Richard, if you're not going to clue me in, please take your phone forty feet back in this motor home."

"Dad, I will gladly move to the back if you will stop bugging me about the doctor!" Off he went, coughing and muttering. I suppose he didn't consider going to the doctor to be a guy thing.

Amplifiers, monitors, microphones, house speakers, and mixing board. A reverb unit for instrumental duets and singing. A huge subwoofer. A wireless mic for trumpet and trombone duets in large auditoriums like Dollywood, the Palace Theater in Crossville, Tennessee, and the Chambersburg, Pennsylvania Middle School. We stored all of our equipment in bins underneath the RV. Above any of the other items, the most important occupant of those bins was Makayla's little red Wal-Mart® cart. It was always right in the front so we were ready for any impromptu shopping event. When we unpacked, we put the little cart reverently into the motor home until we packed up again.

Our daily lives often became dull since we spent hours together riding in the motor home.

"We sure do bounce around a lot," Susan would often joke.

"Divide and Conquer" at Wal-Mart® was always a great way to keep family sanity. Richard and I usually shopped for groceries. That day we switched it up a bit. We pulled up to a Super Wal-Mart® and split into two teams of three: Susan, Kelly and Makayla went food shopping and the men scouted out everything else. We would meet up in the deli section with our carts loaded, so that everyone could choose what he or she wanted for sandwiches.

Richard and I hunted down socks to replace the ones he left in Maine before we began this tour. Baby Richard, an animal cracker in his mouth and crumbs trailing down his green jacket, was in the kiddy seat of the shopping cart, delighted to be part of the guy's outing. We men were impressed at how efficiently we obtained the needed items:

•Diapers - Check.
•Socks - Check.
•Pink flowered skirt size 4 for Makayla - Check.
•Baseball - Check.
•Printer paper - Check.
•Receipt book - Check.

Makayla had the layout of Wal-Mart® memorized and she moved fast to find what we needed. Susan and Kelly had to hotfoot it to keep her in their sights. Kelly told me later she saw a flash of pink and purple and Makayla darting back to her, grabbing her hand, saying, "Here it is, Momma," pointing to the Aisle 8 sign for colds and flu. "Daddy needs medicine, right?" She stood right under the blue "Medicine Cabinet" sign.

After Kelly pulled a bottle off the shelf, Makayla reached up for her hand. "Please may I put that in my cart?" She loved shopping with her mom and grandma. Of course, she always took her miniature red Wal-Mart® cart and carefully added her items to those we put on the checkout counter.

I was proud that my daughter-in-law, in addition to being an integral part of our ministry, took care of two screaming kids and helped around our home on wheels as well.

"There she goes." Susan laughed as she watched Makayla maneuver her cart around the corner to the next aisle. "I asked her to find Kleenex since we are passing colds all around. Get what you need here. I'll watch her."

Right next to the tissues, Makayla abruptly flopped down on the floor.

"What's wrong, honey?" Makayla was sitting cross-legged on the linoleum in the tissue aisle in front of a squished bug.

"He's dead, Grandma," she sniffed. She dissolved into tears while her grandmother stroked her hair. Makayla cares deeply for all of God's creatures, including the creepy-crawling ones.

That night we splurged on a hotel with a swimming pool. This was an unusual indulgence, but Makayla and Richard had begged to go swimming and we longed for luxurious showers outside of a truck stop. Two kids in an RV can easily go stark raving mad, so we always made sure we found a park (especially if it had a ball field), a walking track or playground so we could all get outside, play, walk and relax. Fresh air, green grass, and a breeze rustling through trees were welcome changes from our travelling vehicle. Tonight a swimming pool was just the ticket.

Website post. December 15, 2012:

Makayla went to see her pediatric cardiologist for her fourth yearly checkup. He said that everything looks great and he **can see no more tumors!** They did hook her up to a 24-hour heart monitor to ensure that her heartbeat is normal. Her cardiologist said that if everything looks good next year, she might not have to see him until she is seventeen or eighteen. God continues to watch over her and has His hand on her.

11

Old Time Feeling

"Don't your kids get bored sitting through your concerts?" People swarmed all around Richard asking questions and purchasing CD's, when we paused for coffee and refreshments before that evening's second set. Kelly broke in to save him.

"Actually, Makayla's quite an active, eager participant."

"I like it when they bring us out on stage and introduce us." Makayla stuffed a cookie in her mouth, and then realized she wasn't supposed to talk and eat at the same time. She chewed fast and swallowed hard. "Grandpa asks us to say 'hi' and I make sure my 'hi' is louder than my baby brother, Richard's. Well, actually he can't talk yet because he was just born, so I make up for us both."

She darted off to play with a little girl she had befriended. Kelly and baby Richard were right behind her.

Even though we sing as a trio, we want our listeners to feel as if they know us personally. Four years ago, after Makayla was born, Susan suggested we bring the entire family out on stage so people could meet them. Audiences really enjoyed it, but were always eager to know more about us. Frequently, people would scan the auditorium or church to see where Kelly and the kids were sitting.

I was aware that Makayla knew all the words to our songs, but I had to laugh when I heard she would often ask her mom if the next song on our program was in the hymnal. Nine times out of ten it wasn't, but she would not be deterred. She pretended to look it up in the index. She would then turn to a page with goodness-knows-what-song in the hymnal, and mouth the words of our song as if she were singing along with us.

"The Apple Tree Song" was a big hit at services. While Susan played soft music on the piano, I told the story of a son, alienated from his parents, who desperately wanted them to hang a white cloth on a tree to welcome him home. After my narration, we segued into the song. One of Kelly's jobs was to listen to our balance and signal if we needed to adjust volumes. That day she motioned to Susan to turn down my microphone so our blend would be better.

While we sang, I spied Makayla crawl under a pew. She made her way over to sit next to a lady who was dabbing her eyes with a tissue. She patted the lady's arm. Kelly, holding the baby, crept quietly over to bring Makayla back.

"But Momma, Grandpa's story made that lady cry," Makayla whispered. "I had to go make her feel better."

"That happens a lot on this song, doesn't it, honey?" Kelly laid her free arm across her daughter's shoulders. "But when Daddy and Grandma start singing, people feel better because they realize the song is all about love."

"Okay," Makayla, not quite convinced, said with a tiny frown. The lady turned back to give her a smile and she sparkled one back.

We had asked her every day if she wanted to sing with us at a concert, but she always said no. Just after she turned four, we were setting up the equipment in Manhattan. Makayla said to Susan, "Grandma, I need to talk to Grandpa."

Susan said, "You can talk to Grandpa anytime."

"You sure? He looks pretty busy all the time."

"He's never too busy for his family," Susan encouraged. "Go talk to him."

Gathering our tote bags together, I took a moment to catch my breath in the front of the church after finishing the sound check. Makayla approached me shyly.

"Can I sing with you guys tonight, Grandpa?"

She melted my heart. That night she joined us on "Through It All." I thought it was a good choice, considering all she had been through. For the next three nights after the family introduction, we asked the audience if they would mind if Makayla sang a song with us. It took several moments for the clapping and cheering to die down before we could start.

Four days later, Makayla locked her eyes on mine. "Grandpa, I have to say something serious. I want to sing a different song at our concerts. I mean, I've been doing this one for a while and I think I need a change. Besides it's pretty boring, don't you think?"

Mind you, she had only sung "Through It All" three times, but hey, kids need variety. I bit the side of my cheek to keep from laughing because she sounded like a recording artist negotiating with her manager.

Crouching down in front of her, I rested my hands on her shoulders. "We'll figure out another song, Makayla."

"Oh, I already know which one. I need something peppy, like this." She started snapping her fingers, a skill she had latched on to since Tuesday. Strong and confident, she sang:

I've got a feelin' we're gonna be feelin' that old time
feelin' again.

How could I say no? She was a little shy that night when we announced she would join us on a song. But when the music started with Richard on the verse, Makayla lit up and wiggled her right foot back and forth in time with the music. When it was time for us all to sing the chorus, she planted both feet firmly, raised her microphone, and leaned in toward the audience. She thumped her hand against her hip and showed Susan a new gesture to use. After her father dipped his head toward her on verse two, she tried some fancier footwork. The crowd went wild, especially when she tripped over her own feet. On the last chorus she sang every word with all the vim and vigor one loves to see in a performer.

For those three minutes, we were no longer a trio. We were a quartet!

12

Keep Trusting and Believe

Seventy-six trombones, da da *da* da da! Just like Daddy!" Makayla and I danced hand-in-hand out of the Dutch Apple Theater in Lancaster, Pennsylvania. She let go, trotting out her superb imitation of Richard playing his trombone.

"I'm glad she's geared up. I was ready to drop after driving 800 miles, but giving her this outing thoroughly revived me."

"You only let me drive for an hour. No wonder you're tired," Susan said. "Let's get a shot of this." She grabbed her cell phone while Makayla and I made funny faces for the photograph.

"I liked the lunch almost as much as the songs. Tiny sandwiches, potato salad, and devilled eggs!" Makayla grabbed Susan's hand and skipped on ahead humming away.

She had watched "The Music Man" video many times while riding in the coach. We'd bought tickets six months prior, hoping she'd be delighted to see it live, and we were right. Experiencing a stage production other than our own uplifted us all.

We often drive long stretches, sometimes because my son is what I call "geographically challenged." Richard tries to schedule as many concerts as possible because we do have to make a living and we want to reach as many people as we can. He had slightly misjudged the distance between venues in Illinois to last night's in Pennsylvania. We made it, sang, and crashed immediately into bed. I decided not to give him a hard time, since Makayla loved the show so much.

"That shower has to go." Susan emerged from our tiny shower stall the next morning, toweling her blonde hair.

"It gets me clean just fine," I answered.

"Dell, we don't have enough closet space. We've tried laying out our performance clothes so they stay neat. It's impossible with two small children in a forty-foot home. We could put a bar in there and use it as a performance wardrobe closet. That way I can keep two sets of concert attire wrinkle free and we'll have more toy storage. We'll simply shower in truck stops. We've already learned fuel is cheaper at travel plazas than in towns. I researched it on the Internet. Some are quite elaborate. We earn points when we buy diesel for the coach and that reduces prices on showers and towel rental. We'll just wear flip-flops and take our own soap and shampoo."

"I think I've just been told how this is going to be," I moaned.

"Irksome, yes," Susan admitted, "but it's the best solution." She turned on her hairdryer as if to punctuate the decision-making process.

"Susan, the pastor said he'd unplug the church's stove so we can use their electricity," I said with relief as I climbed into the main section of the motor home and grabbed our heavy-duty extension cord. Borrowing a few volts from our venues was like manna from heaven.

"Good, because I just checked the diesel gauge and it's close to shutting off. I really don't want to sleep in this heat without air conditioning." We were all ready for bed after a rousing concert. I dragged the cord up the back steps of the church. The pastor plugged it in, gave me a pat on the back, and bade us goodnight.

"That should give the refrigerator what it needs for tonight. I'll check the propane in the morning to make sure we can wash dishes," I added when I returned. I slipped off my clothes, carefully hung them in our shower closet, and wrapped my bathrobe around me. I looked forward to a good sleep in a comfortably cool home.

Safety features were built into our motor home. Our air conditioning, microwave, TV, and hot water ran off the generator, which in turn ran on our precious diesel. The generator would shut off automatically when our fuel tank got down to half full. I suppose this was so we'd have enough fuel to drive to a place where we could fill up again. We kept a close eye on that tank for sure. Because of this, Susan's idea of only filling up at less expensive truck stops made perfect sense.

"CAT!" Makayla stuck her finger on the word in the book and raised an eyebrow anticipating Susan's compliment. They squeezed together on the white loveseat near the front of the RV. Susan's computer sat beside them. I knew she had mountains of emails to answer, but Makayla usually won out.

"Your momma is doing a great job of teaching you. Let's find another word to sound out."

"I'd rather read 'Polite As a Princess.' Momma says I have to work on 'please and thank you.' Oh, Grandma, *please* can you read the princess book to me?"

Susan happily complied. I don't know who loved this activity more, the reader or the child. In any event, the book taught manners, an important trait for any age. Since Makayla was very much in the public eye, it pleased us that she wanted her conduct to be proper.

The aroma of hot chicken salad casserole coming from the oven made our mouths water. After reading the princess book three times and instructing her granddaughter to wash up for dinner, Susan gathered salad items from the fridge and sat at the dinette where Kelly homeschooled Makayla.

"I can't believe how fast she's learning," Susan marveled, cutting carrot matchsticks and sprinkling them over a bed of greens.

Kelly placed the casserole on a hot pad and threw down our two need-to-be-replaced potholders. She blew on the finger she just burned on the hot Pyrex dish. "She keeps asking me for more and I'm certainly not going to hold her back."

When dinner was ready, we said grace and the kids ate at the dinette with Kelly supervising. Filling our plates buffet style, the rest of us settled in the adjacent living room. Forks clattered on plates, but no words were uttered, an unusual occurrence in the Hyssong home.

The next morning, I finished tying the bright blue laces on my walking shoes.

"The brighter the better for Grandpa," Makayla had said when she gave them to me for a birthday gift.

Susan and I set out for a community-walking track we noticed when we pulled in last night. Finding alone time was easier said than done. We often went for a walk together around six in the morning while the rest of the family slept.

"I can't believe the courage of that couple who approached us before the service last night." I wrapped my windbreaker tighter around myself to cut off the breeze.

"I saw the husband holding his wife's hand. He could barely meet your eye. What was that about?"

"They heard us sing here last year and said that they almost couldn't come last night. I'm so glad they did."

"Why?"

"Susan, what a powerful chain of events. We sang 'Everything's Fine' last year. It touched them so; they bought the CD. Evidently they lost their little girl four months ago. After she died, they pulled out our CD and played that one song every single morning to start their day with hope. He asked if it would be on last night's program. Of course I said yes. I glanced at them once. They were crying. I really had to pull myself together to get through the rest."

"Bringing comfort. I love that aspect of what we do." Susan nestled her arm in the crook of mine and we walked on in the early morning sun.

A few months later on October 1, 2013, Makayla breezed right by the "Please Wait To Be Seated" sign in the Longhorn Steakhouse and slid into a maroon vinyl-covered booth. Restaurants are her forte. Susan settled into the seat across the table from her, apologizing to the hostess who had already seated Richard and Kelly on the far side of the dining room. Amused, the hostess smiled and placed a booster seat next to Susan for the baby. Makayla and I sat opposite them, my granddaughter rearranging the place settings to her own satisfaction.

We often split up as a family when we ate out. 24/7 in the motor coach sometimes became tense. Tonight was also special because it was Richard and Kelly's wedding anniversary. Longhorn, the site of their first real date, was our number-one choice for family celebrations. One of our followers even sent us a Steakhouse coupon as a gift. Susan and I didn't mind keeping the kids at our table to give our son and his wife some private time.

Makayla beamed. "I'll have a small chocolate milk and he (pointing to twenty-month-old Richard) wants white, please. Thank you!" She flashed Doreen, our waitress, her famous toothy smile.

Makayla folded her legs up under herself in the booth. Doreen returned with both milks, handed out menus, and explained the specials. While we listened, Makayla buried her nose in the menu. She could read most of the items in the children's section because her homeschooling was going so well.

After placing her own order of macaroni and cheese, she announced, "My brother will have the little chicken fingers. The crunchy ones. Thank you. And some catsup, please. Thank you."

Susan and I exchanged triumphant grins. Makayla's princess book was clearly impacting her.

"You said your granddaughter is five? I see a lot of kids

in here. Her speech seems a couple of years ahead of that."

"She spends a good bit of time around adults," I explained.

Susan chose grilled chicken. I stuck with my Longhorn favorite—prime rib. We planned to take leftovers home for the next day's lunch. Makayla organized our menus and handed them back to Doreen. Squirmy time started.

I recognized my signal to quiet her down. Susan had done more than her share by taking the kids to the park earlier, while I taped a segment of my weekly television show, "Joy for the Journey." I drew pictures on the paper tablecloth with crayons from a little glass on the table and asked Makayla to critique them. She speedily jumped into an assessment.

"Grandpa, you can't make a house purple. It has to be brown."

"But purple is one of your favorite colors."

"For dresses, Grandpa, not houses."

"I see." I exchanged the purple crayon for a brown one. Doreen headed to our table with a full tray. I was off the hook.

After our food arrived, Susan and I chatted about upcoming events while she fed Richard. Buried in her mac and cheese, Makayla ignored us.

The kids ate quietly but begged for ice cream the moment plates were cleared. We ordered a sundae and split it four ways. Susan wiped Richard's face clean when we'd finished. We waited for our bill. Makayla became unusually antsy.

At this point in her life, the use of princess movies was most effective. I tapped my granddaughter's arm to get her attention. "Makayla, let's do the prince and princess game."

She immediately settled down eager to play. In her most regal voice she said, “Grandpa, how does the prince bow?” She loved teasing me. We’d played this game countless times in restaurants.

I bowed my head low and extended my right hand to her, palm up. “Ariel, my princess,” I said ceremoniously.

“My prince!” She brightened, fixing her eyes playfully on mine. Tipping her head regally to one side, she laced her hands coyly one above the other on the table. Captivated with our little drama, she finally sat calmly and sipped the rest of her milk. When she noticed they were watching from across the room, she flashed a slow motion princess wave to her parents.

13

Here I Go Again

I marvel that we so easily work together, constantly busy, constantly on-point. We've been together for so long; our professional jobs are well synchronized. Our performance set-up is a joint effort and the three of us go about tasks, not really knowing the jobs of the other two. Wondrously, microphone stands are raised, speakers plugged in, white noise tested, monitors positioned and checked. Kelly sets up the product table. We change into performance clothes and The Hyssongs are ready to take the stage.

I've already explained how Richard and I work as a team. As promised, I'll tell you about Susan and Kelly. Aside from all of their domestic and family duties, both contribute to the business aspect as well. Susan sends out confirmations, writes receipts for contributions, and works with Kelly on CD cover design. Kelly maintains our website, sends out posters, and assists Richard with his radio program. Dividing up jobs and not overlapping on tasks helps us keep our sanity. We may be exhausted most of the time, but we love what we do. Here's a bit more about life in our home on wheels. I know you are all dying to hear this part but are too polite to ask.

It was late when we pulled away from the church.

"I'm hungry," Richard yelled from the back of the coach. Before long everyone was asking me to stop for some food.

When I heard Makayla's "I'm starved," I knew it was time to pull into a fast-food restaurant.

Richard and Susan took our orders, jumped out, and started out the door while Kelly went into the back to get the kids ready for bed. I changed into old clothes to drive in.

The entrance to the fast food restaurant was locked, so Susan and Richard walked around to the drive-thru window. Susan waved me to come over, so I jumped out of the coach and started toward her and Richard.

"No!" She cupped her hands around her mouth and yelled. "Bring the motor home. They won't serve us unless we are driving a vehicle."

I jumped back behind the wheel and pulled the forty-foot coach up to the drive-thru. Our diesel engine rumbled into the speaker.

"May I help you?" asked the worker. Richard and Susan, still outside, placed our order with the person on the other end of the speaker. Deciding we were set, I pulled ahead toward the parking lot. You should have seen the worker's reaction when Richard and Susan walked up to the window to get the food.

We laughed for the next half hour as we ate, retold and relived the experience.

Scouting out eating establishments at 9:30 PM was

a challenge. We customarily ate our main meal in the middle of the day. Susan would make lasagna and sloppy joes in advance to stock our freezer. Sometimes we'd be too busy to remember to thaw them out, or we just didn't feel like working that hard, especially if we had concerts morning and night in the same day. On those occasions we were all famished after the second concert. That's when our food choices were largely determined by what food establishments stayed open late into the evening.

"Dad, you're exhausted. I'll drive."

I love my son, but when he drove, I'd grit my teeth. I moved over to the passenger seat, gripping the door handle before falling asleep. I've always been a white-knuckle driver, but when Richard drove my whole hand turned numb. We had sung a six PM concert in Maryville, Tennessee, and had a thirteen-hour drive ahead of us to arrive the next day in Birdsboro, Pennsylvania. We planned to drive all night to save the better part of tomorrow for food shopping and preparation, washing and ironing clothing, and confirming all of our upcoming services in Lancaster County. At the top of Richard's list was a daddy/daughter date at the local Chinese restaurant.

I was drifting off to sleep, thinking of the next day's projects, when I heard our tires going over rumble strips. And then again. *Three times and you're out, son.*

Richard is a good driver, but his mind runs a million miles an hour. To be honest, he doesn't focus on his driving as much as I'd like. I got up to kick him out of the driver's seat.

He raised an eyebrow. "Sorry Dad, I was thinking about which radio DJs I need to call in the morning. I sure hope they'll chart our new song." He noted my lack of enthusiasm and quickly made a beeline to join Kelly who was already asleep.

"I'll keep you company." Susan yawned and slid into the passenger seat. She does this because she's afraid I'll nod off and I love her all the more for it. We planned the next day.

"Let's use the Flying J at exit 323 for showers. It's so much cleaner, and the next town has a decent Laundromat," she said sleepily.

Many people would ask me if Makayla and Richard minded traveling. That's a tough question. Honestly, can you imagine keeping two kids happy in a motor home?

Normally, one adult napped, another drove (me), and the other two took care of the kids. While the children took afternoon naps, Susan, Kelly and Richard were working on their computers.

When Kelly wasn't homeschooling Makayla at the dinette, Susan often played board games and did puzzles with her. We'd play DVD's for both kids, but reading books topped the list. One day during rush hour, I overheard a pretend game, which kept me calm while I was passing trucks on the highway in the rain.

Susan knelt on the tan leather sofa near the front of the motor home with Makayla standing on the cushion next to her. They watched out the window and made up stories.

"I see a little green car and a little yellow house." Makayla pointed as we drove by.

"Who do you think lives in that little yellow house, Makayla?"

"Hm." Makayla enjoyed getting into this game. "There's a grandma like you and she's baking."

"I smell cinnamon buns," Susan said.

"Do you think we could eat some? With milk?"

"She's probably making them for her own family. When we get home, how about you and I bake brownies?"

"I love making brownies!"

Flour on the floor. Flour on the chairs. Flour on the counters. We had reached Rockport the night before and Susan rapidly made good on her promise. I know cooking can be messy, but I'd never seen the amount of flour Susan and Makayla spread all over the kitchen that day.

"Good, you're home. Dell, go get that little red mini vac from the motor coach, would you?" Susan asked, brushing white stuff out of her hair with her fingers. "She decided to play with it," she said with a sheepish smile, showing me her white powdered hand.

When I finished vacuuming, Susan was giving instructions.

"Three jobs, Makayla, and three jobs only. You spray the cooking spray in the pan. After I measure the water you pour it in. I take care of the flour, understand?"

Five-year-old Makayla piped up, "Grandma, you forgot my best job. The counting."

"Go give Grandpa a hug for cleaning up our mess and then you can count while I stir." Taking out her wooden spoon from the drawer, Susan explained to me, "I have to stir the brownie batter fifty times."

Sensing my cue to get out of the kitchen, I gave a quick nod, tucked the vacuum under my arm, and backed quietly into the living room.

"48, 49, 50! Ready for the oven," Makayla said with relish. "Okay, Grandma, pour it into the pan and I get to smooth the top."

When her mother came to pick her up two hours later, Makayla proudly handed her a tin of freshly baked brownies to take home for the family.

Life onboard went pretty smoothly, but unforeseen catastrophes occasionally cropped up. I did my best to keep the motor home in optimum shape. Recently it had a general maintenance including oil and filter changes. We put new brake drums and shoes on the back. I thought we were set. I'd hoped so because the bank account was low. Just to be sure, we checked in with our mechanic for a routine look over.

"Oh, no," he said, moving his creeper from the back to the front under the vehicle. "This drag link has too much play in it."

The drag link, he explained, connects the steering wheel to the wheels. If he hadn't found the problem, we could have been out on the highway with no steering capacity at all.

"How long will it take to order a new part?" I asked. We needed to get on the road within hours to reach our concert, planned for more than a year, in Rhode Island.

After he checked online, he informed me, "Oregon has one. Maybe a week to ten days until it arrives."

We asked him to order it and rushed to change gears. We packed our equipment into our trailer and hitched it up to the light green Windstar® van.

"I was really hoping Kelly and the kids could come

with us." Richard's disappointment was obvious but it couldn't be helped.

Two miles from home the engine light came on in the Windstar® van. We drove right back to our mechanic. After hooking it up to the computer, he said, "You need a new coil and it'll take me an hour to fix it."

We didn't have an hour. We ran the same vehicle back home and hooked the trailer up to our second Windstar®. Pressed for time, Susan, Richard and I again made headway toward Rhode Island. Fifty miles from home, we smelled something funny.

"It's antifreeze," I said, after I got out of the car and watched green liquid snaking down the street. On the other side of the road I spied a new dealership. Eager to help, they put a mechanic on the problem. He changed the leaking hose. We always allowed plenty of time when traveling to engagements, but it was getting tight.

New pipe installed, we drove an hour and a half. We still had two-and-a-half hours to reach our destination when the car started bouncing. People in passing vehicles tooted their horns and pointed toward our trailer. Richard peered out the window and saw parts of our trailer wheel flying off.

"We've only put a hundred miles on those new wheels, right, Dad?" he asked.

We'd never hit a situation like this before. The only other time in our career that we cancelled was when we'd heard the dreadful news about Makayla's heart.

All good intentions and planning can't defend against multiple vehicle breakdowns. We waited on the side of the road for a wrecker. Richard quickly called the church and posted on Facebook:

October 28, 2014

We are sorry to say we have had to cancel tonight's concert. We are currently on the side of a road. We apologize to all our friends in Rhode Island for tonight's cancellation. We will be resuming our concerts tomorrow night.

After three hours the wrecker arrived.

"We've had a bad day," Richard told the driver.

Putting things into perspective, the wrecker driver responded, "I pick up a lot of vehicles where no one gets out alive. I'd say you are having a great day!"

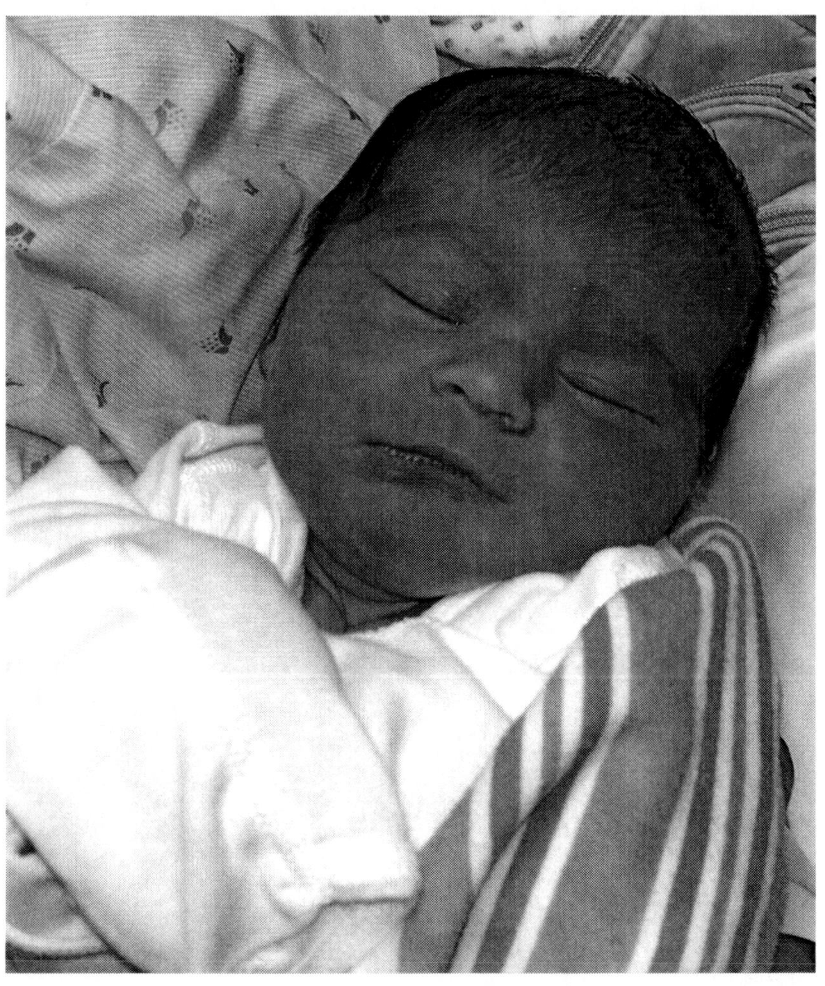

One day old

One day old with Dad

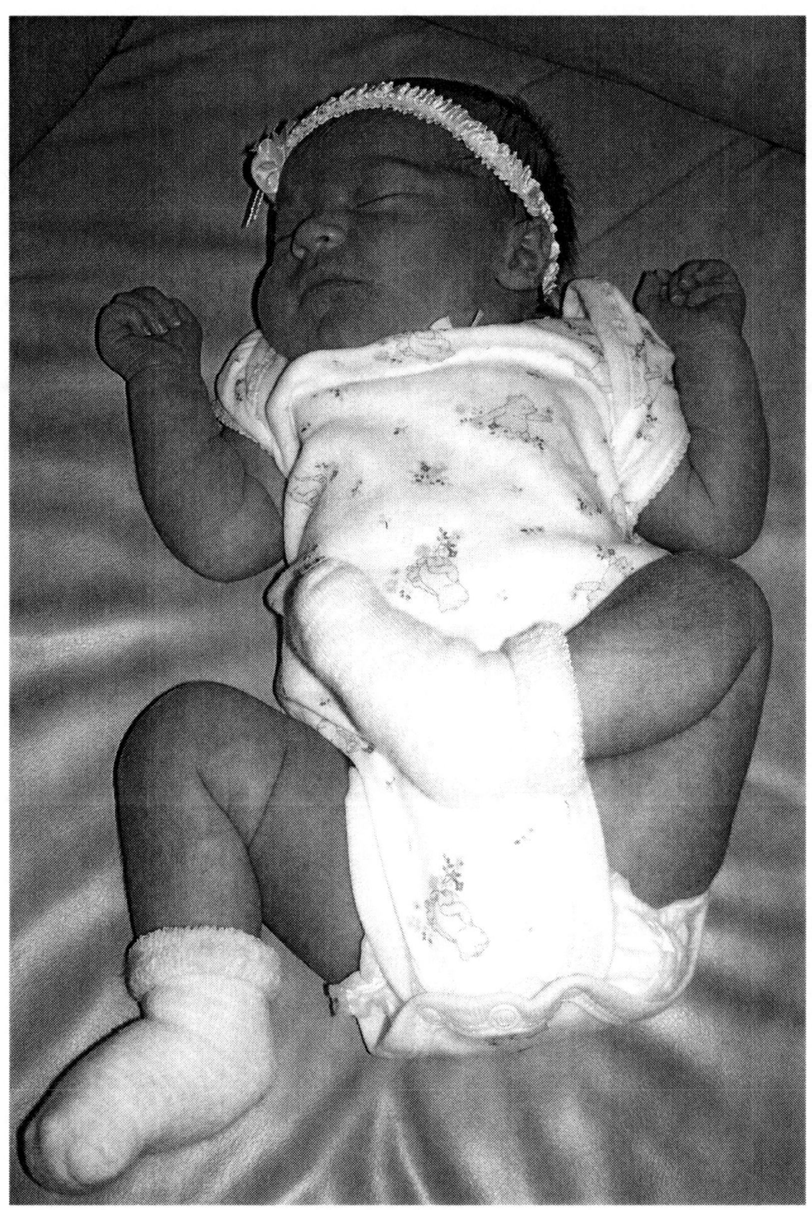

Sweet dreams
First day home

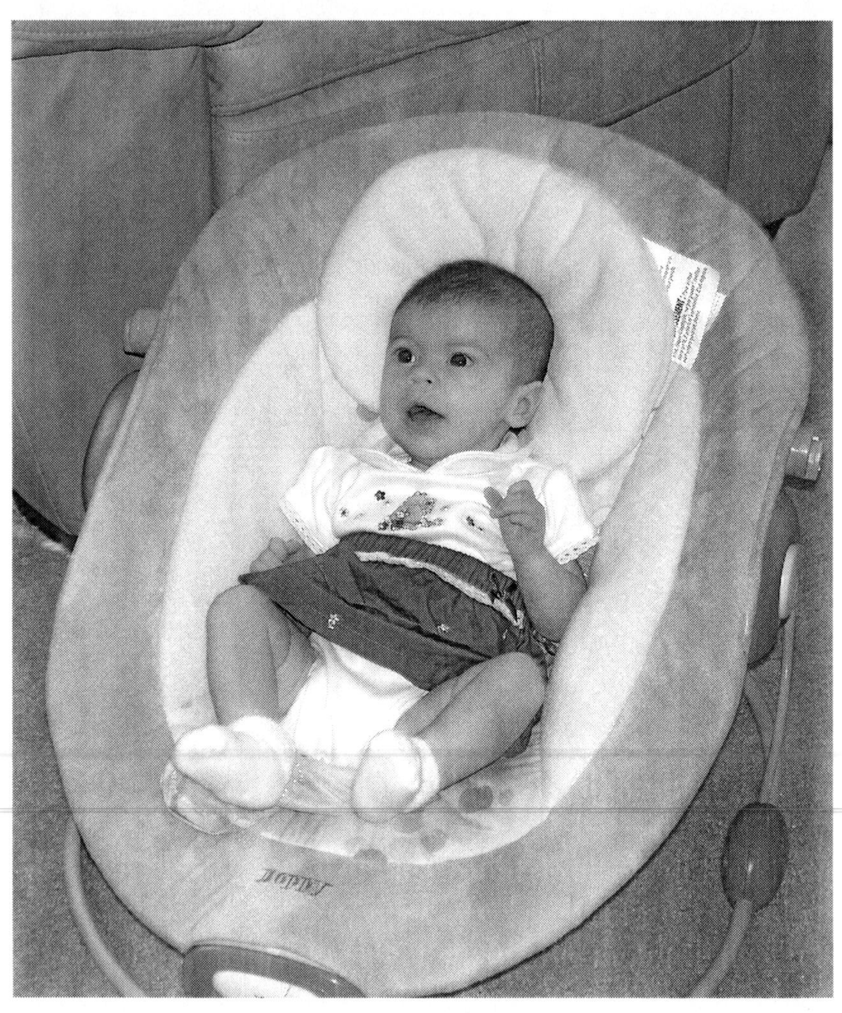

Makayla imitates her dad

14

Through It All

"Hi, Mr. Yoki. Remember me from last year?" Makayla swished the skirt of her pink polka dot dress back and forth as she followed her father down the stairs. We were setting up in Maynard, Massachusetts. Makayla insisted her father needed help "hooking up the plug" on the sub woofer.

"I sure do, Little Miss. How's it going? Will you be singing tonight?" He clambered up the stairs, arms full of cookie trays, toward the social hall where we would greet friends after the concert.

"Makayla, that man's name is Mr. Joki, not Mr. Yoki," her father corrected her.

After the concert, Richard and I were manning the display table upstairs. Mr. Joki stopped by for a chat.

"I loved it when Makayla called me Yoki. No one's called me that since I was a kid in Finland. I explained the Finnish pronunciation of my name to her when I saw you last year. What a memory your little girl has!"

Makayla remembers everyone she meets. She loves people, period. Young and old alike are drawn to her like a magnet. Although she has children her age as friends at home, she tends to be more comfortable around older children and adults. Spending so much time with us is probably a contributing factor. Many people call her an “old soul.” My granddaughter, the girl with wisdom beyond her years. Every day with her is a gift.

While we are all riding in one car, Richard confers with a radio producer. Susan, sharing the second seat with Makayla, accepts a reservation for our upcoming “Experience of a Lifetime,” planned for Rockport in 2015. In between calls, Makayla sings at the top of her lungs to pass the time. The baby is crying over goodness knows what in the rear with Kelly trying to console him. I am driving, as usual. Yes, it is my choice. You’ve probably noticed I am a control freak in that sense. Ironically, all noise in our vehicle stops simultaneously. Richard cracks a joke.

We all laugh and relax. People think Richard is very funny. Indeed he is, not only on stage and but also as we travel. Sometimes that is exactly what we need to keep going day after day. As you can see, our lives can become crazy. No matter. We love the mission given to us.

God has been good to us. As of October 2014, our song, “I Was Blind, But Now I See” is #7 on the Singing News chart. We jumped out of our seats when, at the 2014 National Quartet Convention of Southern Music Artists, we were announced as Favorite New Trio. Within our industry, we are known for Southern Gospel music, but that is not our only genre. We also perform traditional hymns, Christmas music, brass duets, and piano duets. We regularly interject humor to lighten the spirit of our concerts. Radio has really embraced our family and we are thrilled that our music is making a difference in people’s lives. We look forward to our Western Caribbean Cruise in 2015 where we will minister afloat.

If you know our music prior to reading this book, you've probably noticed the chapter headings are actual songs we have recorded. Our music strengthens us, as do our everyday lives and laughter. We genuinely enjoy being together on stage and off.

As much as we love playing with our audiences, they give it back to us good. After we do our first set tonight, I ask if anyone wants to hear Makayla join us on a song.

"Woo-hoo! We want Makayla!"

Cameras flash, feet stomp, people cheer wildly. After Makayla sings she gets a standing ovation. Clearly, she eats up the appreciation.

"Really?" Richard feigns dismay with shoulders drooping. "The Hyssongs just gave you twenty minutes of quality music. Makayla sang for two minutes. Two. She gets all this attention? No standing ovation for the trio?"

A guy from the audience pipes up.

"She's way cuter than you are, Richard!"

We can't argue with that.

15

Moment by Moment

Exciting and rewarding seem fitting descriptions for our time in family ministry. God has always pulled us together. Unity has been our calling card through all of our difficult times. Our love for each other is profound, intensified by Makayla's health issues. As a family we've learned that our greatest spiritual growth happens when we pass through trials and accept unanswered questions. God surrounds us in every way and in every circumstance.

The Hyssong's music is bigger than we are as individuals or as a trio. People all over the world have bolstered us with prayer and support. We've needed both to buoy our spirits and strengthen our faith in God. When we sing, we pray that we may be channels of His love, empowering and blessing everyone who hears us. We want each concert we do to point people to God, the only One true provider of the help we all need.

Makayla is just one example of God's blessings to us. The joy she brings to our family is inestimable. She continues to sing with us at concerts, understanding that she can bow out at any time. Today, all twenty-two tumors in her heart are completely gone. Can we call her recovery miraculous? We have no doubts at all. For Susan, Kelly, Richard and I, it is.

She is doing great and we are excited about the future. However, like you, we never know what tomorrow holds. She will have tests for the rest of her life. We are enjoying every single minute together. May we all live each day to the fullest because only God knows our tomorrows.

Moment by moment Makayla's heart beats on.

Moment by moment she fills our hearts with joy.

Never a trial that He is not there.
Moment by moment, we're under His care.

Time for lunch

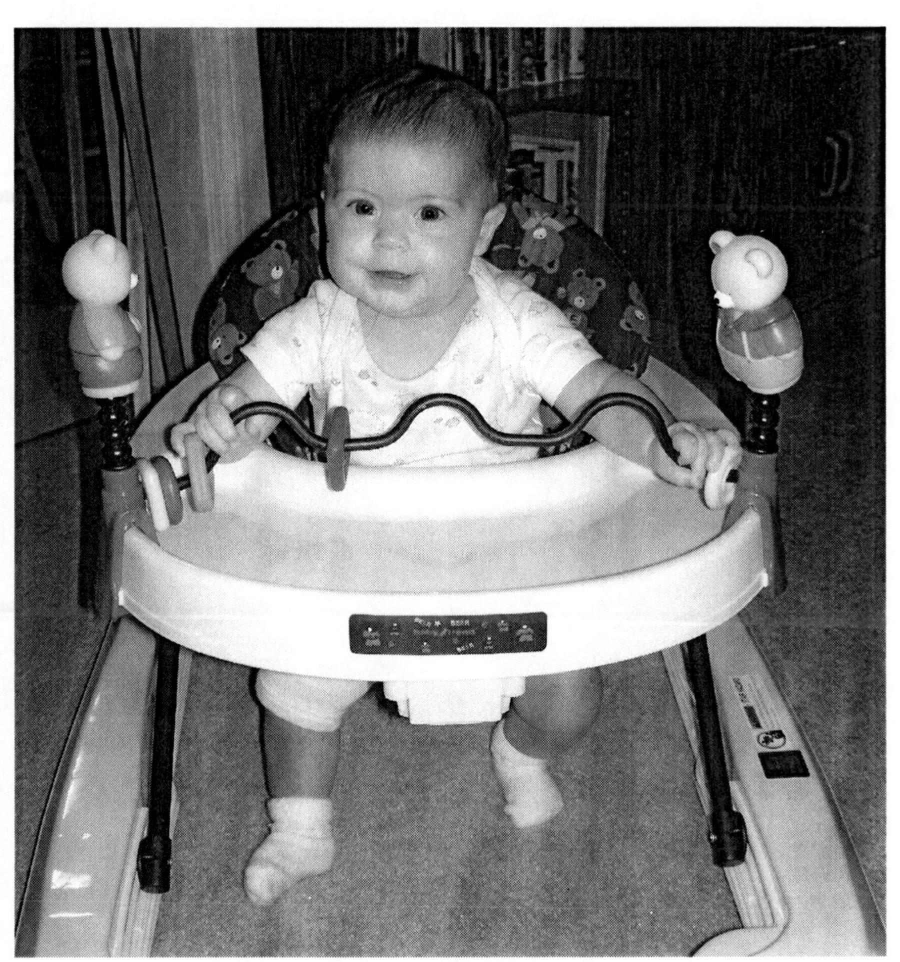

Look out, here I come!

Is this too loud?

Loves music
One Year Old

Marco... Polo...

This is the life!

Time to play!

Serving tea

I love books!

Mery Christmas - at 2 and 1/2

Photo by Gail Shelby-Vision Photography

Two of a kind

Proud sister

Giddyup!

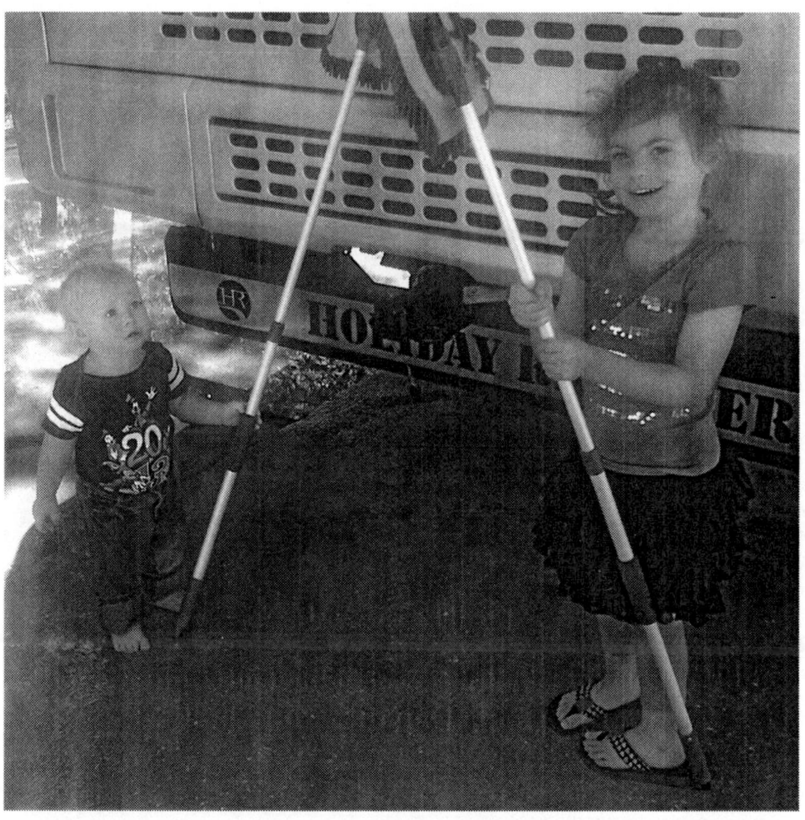

Washing the motorhome with my brother. Where did our parents go?

First time to sing

Richard, Kelly,
Makayla, and Richard

Photo by Paul Wharton - Wharton Photography

Best Buddies

Photo by Paul Wharton - Wharton Photography

Grandpa with Makayla, Richard, and their friend Pluto

Dell, Susan, Richard, Kelly, Richard, and Makayla

Photo by Paul Wharton - Wharton Photography

Author's Note

In 1974 I boarded a plane heading from Chicago O'Hare to Newark International Airport. Two months before finishing my Master of Music degree from Northwestern University, I faced an interview for a position as Instructor of Voice at a private New Jersey college. When I arrived on campus, I met the chair of the music department. He informed me that as part of my interview I would give a voice lesson, under observation, to one of the college's students. The student that walked into the studio that day was Dell R. Hyssong Jr.

Subsequently, I was offered the position. In addition to private vocal instruction, I taught courses in theory, choral conducting, and diction. I also conducted the Concert Choir, taking them on tour. Dell Hyssong studied voice with me for two years. I have fond memories of his resonant, rich baritone voice, his musicality, and his sense of humor. I also taught his future wife, Susan. When they married in 1976, I was honored when they asked me to sing at their wedding.

My life took some turns and soon I lost track of Dell and Susan Hyssong. Forty years later, in May 2014,

I noticed a poster in my church advertising a concert. I recognized Dell's grin before reading the announcement of a concert to be held in town the following week. After looking the Hyssong's up on the Internet, I discovered they are a prominent family singing trio. We emailed back and forth that week. Our reunion at the performance was a gift from God.

For some time Dell had wanted to put on paper the story of his granddaughter, Makayla, and her fight with Tuberous Sclerosis. I'd already authored a historical fiction novel, *Crestmont*, and written over a hundred articles and book reviews, so I offered to help out. *Makayla's Heart: Moment by Moment* is the product of our collaboration.

I want to express my deep appreciation to the entire Hyssong family who granted me interviews, sent me countless recordings relating their experiences during Makayla's early years, and hosted my husband and me at their home in Rockport, Maine. As I came to understand the uncertainties and struggles they went through and the faith that sustained them, my respect for them intensified one-hundred-fold.

I thank T. C. McMullen and Star Publish for their expertise and guidance. I am indebted to Laurel L. Septer, Linda Williamson and Kristen, a friend, who read the rough manuscript, giving me insights and encouragement. Lastly my husband, Ernie Whitehouse, the guy in the green recliner, never failed to support me in countless ways through the writing process.

—Holly Weiss, 2015 www.hollyweiss.com

Holly Weiss
Author

Holly Weiss, author of the award-winning novel *Crestmont*, is a private vocal instructor, retired professional singer, and a member of the National Association of Teachers of Singing. She has taught singers in her private studio since 1974. One voice led to another when Weiss transitioned from public singing to writing in 2006. Her extensive literary experience and love of reading have turned her into a cutting-edge reviewer of books. She reviews for Book of the Month Club and EzineArticles.com.

Weiss's debut novel, *Crestmont*, a historical fiction gem set in 1920s Pennsylvania, was received to great acclaim. Reader Views awarded *Crestmont* first place for their 2011 Awards for Books. *Crestmont* is available at major online stores in soft cover and eBook formats.

In 2011, the Greater Newburg Symphony Orchestra commissioned Weiss to write poetic verses for Bizet's orchestral suite, *Children's Games, Opus 22,* a project she found gratifying because it combined her musical and writing skills.

Holly Weiss earned a Master of Music from Northwestern University in 1974. In 2007, she was listed in Who's Who in America. She contracted polio in 1952 and is now an advocate for Eradicate Polio. Through the years she has supported several children through Compassion International. She lives Connecticut with her husband, Ernie Whitehouse. Even though dealing with Post Polio Syndrome, she leads an active life.

Visit her at www.hollyweiss.com.

"*Crestmont* is a fine and riveting read for historical fiction fans, highly recommended."

—Midwest Book Review

"Weiss has chosen to 'sing' something she truly loves... a historical novel for those who want to retreat to a 1920s free of grit, like Weiss's smooth, efficient prose.

—Daphne Kalotay, author of Russian Winter and Sight Reading

"Weiss demonstrates her refined artistic skill, capably translated from song to pen..."

—Janet Furness, PhD, Ramapo University

"Holly Weiss knows how to paint with words."

—Dorothy Diemel, Utica, NY

Dell R. Hyssong, Jr.
Author

Dell Hyssong, Jr. sings baritone; his wife, Susan (alto); and son, Richard (tenor) for the award-winning gospel music group, The Hyssongs. Full-time musicians, they bring their Christ-centered music to the public performing over 250 concerts annually. They were voted "Favorite New Trio" by the subscribers of Singing News Magazine in 2014, and several of their songs have charted on Southern Gospel's Top 40. Dell airs a weekly television show, *Joy for the Journey* and writes a monthly column by the same name in *Christian Voice Magazine*.

An ordained minister, Dell has a Master's Degree in Ministry, and served as a senior pastor for more than 25 years. He is a popular speaker at churches, conferences, and on college campuses sharing his heart for evangelism and Christian music. The Hyssongs tour nationally and internationally. As a native of the state of Maine, Dell loves lobster and spending time on the rugged, rocky coastline when they are home.

Dell's greatest joy this side of heaven is his family. Dell and Susan have been happily married since 1976. In 2005, Richard married Kelly – Makayla was born in 2008 and

Richard IV in 2012. The Hyssongs hope you are blessed by *Makayla's Heart: Moment by Moment*– her miracle and their story.

You can reach Dell through www.thehyssongs.com.

Sources

Americaner, Susan. *We Are Happy*. New York, NY: Disney Enterprises, Inc., 2012.

Downing, Ann. "Stay Close to Me." 2003, *God Looking In*. Copyright (2003) by Ann Downing. Reprinted with permission.

Hinson, Kenny. "Old Time Feeling." 1984,*Lift the Roof Off*. Copyright 1984 by Kenny Hinson.

Lagronegro, Melissa. *Polite As a Princess*. New York, NY: Random House Children's Books, 2006.

Webster, Daniel Whittle/Moody, May Whittle. "Moment by Moment." 1893. Public Domain.

The Hyssongs Biography

Dell, Susan, and Richard Hyssong travel full-time as the award-winning Hyssongs. Their energetic ministry combines family vocal harmony, humor, and brass instruments (trumpet and trombone) to delight audiences with their Christ-centered message, shared through the powerful medium of music. The family's classical music background, along with their harmony and specific chord structures, lend them a unique sound that has made quite an impact on audiences.

The group has been singing together as a family for more than 18 years. In that time, the Hyssongs have received many accolades for their quality, inspirational Southern Gospel sound. The group was awarded the Singing News Fan Award for 2014 Favorite New Trio at the National

Quartet Convention, Pigeon Forge, Tennessee. They have consistently placed songs on the Southern Gospel Radio charts. They have had many top 40 songs, three top twenty songs, and most recently their song "I Was Blind But Now I See" reached #7 on the Singing News Radio Chart. The Hyssongs were the cover story in the March 2015 Singing News Magazine and have been featured in Christian Voice Magazine several times. Recently they were listed among ten artists by Absolutely Gospel.com as ones to watch in 2015. The group has also been featured on Paul Heil's "The Gospel Greats" radio program.

The Hyssongs perform at more than 250 events each year throughout the United States and Canada. They minister in churches, auditoriums, and on Gospel singing cruises, as well as on television and radio. The Hyssongs have had the opportunity to sing to an audience of over 12,000 people on the Main Stage at the National Quartet Convention, perform at Renfro Valley's All-Night Sing, and annually perform at Dollywood. Through Compassion International, the group has also been privileged to visit El Salvador, Central America.

(207)751-1966
www.thehyssongs.com Email: dell@thehyssongs.com

Believe

1. You'd Better Believe That It's True
2. Oh How They'll Shine
3. There's Still Room, There's Still Hope, There's Still Time
4. I've Got A Love
5. Lead Me To The Rock
6. While This Blessing's Being Made
7. Choose Life
8. Death Could Not Hold Him
9. The Well
10. The King Is Coming

Right Time, Right Place

1. It's The Right Time
2. I Still Believe
3. I Was Blind But Now I See
4. Home
5. He Touched Me
6. No Matter How Far
7. Still Blessed
8. God's Been Good
9. God Is Great
10. A Matter of Time

Trusting

1. I Was Created To Worship The Lord
2. Through It All
3. When I Get Carried Away
4. Thinking About Going Home
5. Is It Just Me
6. God's In Control
7. Keep Trusting and Believe
8. Everything's Fine
9. I'd Rather Have Jesus
10. I Sing The Mighty Power of God

Blessed

1. We've Come To Worship
2. I Choose The Lord
3. Oh What A Name
4. I'll Stand Up and Say So
5. There's Something About That Name
6. I've Got A Feeling
7. Little Prayers
8. Don't Give Up
9. Old Time Feeling
10. We Are So Blessed

Live DVD

1. Introduction By Paul Heil of The Gospel Greats
2. I Sing The Mighty Power of God
3. Is It Just Me
4. Majesty
5. I'm Expecting A Miracle
6. Everything's Fine
7. Old Time Feeling
8. Oh What A Name
9. The Apple Tree
10. When We All Get To Heaven – Piano Duet
11. I'll Fly Away
12. I'd Rather Have Jesus
13. The King Is Coming
14. Old Time Feeling Encore
15. BONUS CUT: Thinking About Going Home Music Video

The Hyssongs Music Order Form

Project	Media	Price	Qty.	Total
NEW! Believe	CD	$15.00	#	$
Right Time, Right Place	CD	$15.00	#	$
The Hyssongs Live DVD	DVD	$20.00	#	$
Trusting	CD	$15.00	#	$
Blessed	CD	$15.00	#	$
Christmas	CD	$15.00	#	$
Favorite Hymns	CD	$15.00	#	$
Brass: A Collection of Praise	CD	$15.00	#	$
Children's Songs Vol. 1	CD	$15.00	#	$
Rejoice	CD	$15.00	#	$
Celebrate Christmas	CD	$15.00	#	$
			Shipping & Handling	$2.50
			GRAND TOTAL	**$**

Name______________________ **Address**______________________________

Telephone____________________ ______________________________

Thank you for your order. Please send this form along with a check to

The Hyssongs
P.O. Box 525
Rockport, ME 04856

OR

Call 207-751-1966
with a credit card

www.thehyssongs.com **dell@thehyssongs.com**